The Po Change

CW00860347

Fifty poems exploring the light and shadow side of change

by Paul Levy

Catten Publishing

Introduction

A lot of people find it difficult to change. Change can make us happier or sadder, more or less satisfied. It can bring about disappointment or delight, excitement or boredom.

Over the last thirty years I have been working in the realm of change – with individuals, groups, organisations and communities. I also work in the artistic world, in theatre. My books are usually non-fiction. Over those three decades I've also written poetry – to help me and others make sense of and explore change. A friend recently said I ought to publish those poems. So here are some of them. The book might be a nice present to give to someone who is going through a significant change.

You can read them all straight through. This is also a book to dip into. Open it at any page and you'll find something that might help you reflect on change in your life. There are many different styles and I haven't organised them in any particular way.

You can read a poem and not always understand every word. You may feel you don't "get it". Yet poetry is something we can "get" on different levels. Imagine you have a challenge facing you - at home or at work.

Use your intuition and find a poem among the fifty here. You might be drawn to the title, or even the length or shape of the poem. Read the poem - to yourself, or perhaps aloud. Let the poem impress itself on you.

You might understand every word in a poem. Or it might have a less definable impact.

Sometimes a poem can be like a key that unlocks a door to understanding and even help you to find an answer, a solution, or you might just end up with different, better questions.

The Poetry of Change

There is a short commentary at the end of each poem which tells you why I wrote the poem, or what I think might be valuable or important about it. You could skip those and just read the poems. There are also questions in the commentary to help you reflect on some of the themes that arise out of the poems. Take some time to reflection those questions and, where relevant to you, apply them to changes going on in your life.

I hope you enjoy these poems and gain benefit from them. I certainly gained a lot of personal value from writing them.

Paul Levy
Brighton, UK, 2015

The Poems

1. Brighton Sea Walk

Will you walk away again,

Bag, too heavy, swinging down,

Along the promenade, away

Towards the place where the sun sometimes sets?

Will you walk away aimful, aimless,

Towards a place called Away from You ?

The Ice Cream Man is closing now,

The candy floss is packed inside,

The whirly windmills stilled under lock and key;

And you walk.

You walk.

You.

I wrote this poem after a witnesses two people, a man and a woman in a fierce argument. Suddenly she tore away from him and started walking away. He stayed where he was. It was the end of the day. Was it the end of a relationship? She kept walking. He didn't move. Yet I felt that the distance that grew between them was necessary then for anything to be resolved later.

The Poetry of Change

2. Explode Poem

How to explode a situation:
Put dynamite under the assumptions.
Light the fuse.
Pour acid upon the elements and
Watch their appalling interaction
Fizzle Away.

With a new Uzi, rapid-fire all of the
Deeds and Motives until they Shatter.
Sear the Sensitivities with a flame-gun
And finally, frazzle the beliefs and values
With a killing look.

The fuse then reaches its destination and
BOOM! BOOM! BOOM!
The Assumptive base cracks and the whole
Edifice Collapses.
Clear the ground,
And begin again.

I wrote this poem to look at why change – personal or organisational – seem to stall so often. Does change sometimes just need a good old explosion, levelling the ground, to enable us to start all over again?

(An Uzi is a type of rapid-fire gun)

The Poetry of Change

3. Gravity

Come,
Rest your gravity
Upon this floating
Spacelessness.
This is no void,
But a realm where
All possibility floats up
To meet the heavy falling
Of your thinking.

Like Dandelion wishes,
They'll fly to meet you,
And kiss each broken thought
Into a dancing swirl of lightness.

A poem I wrote to explore the themes of gravity and lightness. Sometimes our heaviness can be healed and lessened by the lightness of another person.

4. Plop Poem

This day fell,
Like the Pope,
To Hell.
Plop!
Then suddenly my troubles
Popped, like bubbles.

An irreverent poem that looks at how change can be instantaneous.
We always need big change to take a lot of time!

5. Bamboo

I am building a bamboo
Paper tower of cards
Towards you,
You keep torching it with
A look.

Look, the glowing embers
Of leaf-fall paper catch
In my hair and set me
A-light.

Light as a feather I am
Burning for you and
Building Another bamboo
Paper tower of cards
Towards you,
You keep torching it with
A look.

Look, the glowing embers…

A poem about reaching and connecting. Our connections with each are fragile and can be easily broken. Sometimes we have to try again, and again...

6. Valentine

Do you know
The skill you have?
How you unwrap my
Sadness like an
Unwanted Present?

So easily you
Do it. By just
Being, not doing,
The paper turns
Translucent and,
Without showing,
You show the way.

Each salted tear
Caught so skilfully
In your hands.
You cup me and I
am safe for a moment
Held, by easy
Formation
Of all that you are.

A Valentine poem, but also a poem that celebrates the value and uniqueness of the "other" and why we can be constantly surprised and delighted by those in our lives.

7. Still Your Boat

Still your boat
In these, my waters,
This cove of yellow-gold;

Rest your thoughts
In calmness, cool,
Where gentle waves of peace enfold.

The importance of creating came and finding those spaces where we live that allow us
time and place to relax, let go, recharge and reflect.
Change requires pauses as well as action.

8. Summer Days

Your description of his broken soul,
His nasty deeds, and scheming ways,
His vanity and urge to own
Will haunt these rainy, summer days.

Your cry for help, to once be free,
To be released from a trap so sure;
You said "He hides behind his eyes";
Such "love" is locked behind a door.

I knew that you'd be drawn back in,
But every single word you said
Betrays the fact you do not love
This broken soul, that love is dead.

You'll act so well, from sympathy.
You'll try to remake history.
And all will circle round once more,
Then pain will cut you to the core.

Your description of his broken soul,
His nasty deeds, and scheming ways,
His vanity and urge to own
Will haunt these rainy, summer days.

Sometimes winter can sit in the heart of our summer. Even with the sun high and warm overhead, it's possible to be trapped in a cold, dark place. Even as our friends smile and enjoy life all around us, we can be trapped in the chill.

The Poetry of Change

9. You'd Love This Rain

You'd love this rain;
Mayday, spring day rain.
You'd love this café;
Under parasol, made for sunshine;
Shielding us from the rain.
These are Sussex drops,
Delightfully soaking,
Wetting a nose I long to kiss;
Sea-rain, salty, like tears,
Cleansing, like Love's falling story.
Two forks, one slice of
Caramel Apple Granny;
These pigeons adore the splashes,
And I love to watch you
Watching me, watching them.
You'd love this rain; it's neither
Cold nor too warm; it's a Sussex
Rain, that celebrates the peace
Of the Middle Way; not compromise,
But the Courage of Calm.
Like Pooh's corner, and dear Ratty.
In England, the sun never hides;
It steps back, for thought to quicken
In Spring-tide showers, though sometimes
It sparkles in this jewel-bright water,
Reminding us: Your light, though
Hidden, perhaps even from you;
Is never far. You'd love this rain.

A poem about the healing effect of rain. Sometimes we find change in ourselves when we step physically into the changes in the weather outside.

10. Again

Again I saw you kiss a hand,
A hand that belonged to a head;

A head that gave birth to a tongue
That wished me dead.

This is one of the darkest poems I've ever written. It's about how we can be entirely unaware of the darker feelings of other people, especially if they are dressed in the disguise of warmth and smiles.

11. Demoniser

Once a little demon
Is placed between the ears,
All around are gripped to core
By horror-knotted fears.

Love becomes a badge with
Pin stuck deep inside the heart,
Parading hate-less fury, tarted
Like a candy cart.

And when the poltergeist
Has been allowed the spirit's home,
The ones who claim domain of God
Allow their pain to roam.

It wanders over fields of love
Transformed to opposite,
And dressed in garb of justice
Hurls itself into the pit.

A quirky poem about demonising and demonisers. Why do we demonise other people? Are you demonising another person or a group? Do you need to correct a distorted picture some else holds of you?

12. The Kettle

In search of words to move a soul,
I find a bloody gaping hole.
In search of verse to exorcise,
My muse from bed refused to rise.

I wish to find a dirge that shakes,
A stanza phrase that boldly wakes,
That opens eyes, and confronts lies,
But every single effort dies.

There are no words to heal this thing,
No lines to pen, no notes to sing.
For while the demon sits between,
There are no humans to be seen.

So I will do what English men,
Were taught to do from age of ten;
To sigh, in knowing all is gone,
And gently put the kettle on.

I wrote this is a very "English", post-war style.
Sometimes when situations become paralysed, when there's more darkness than light,
we have to take a breathe and start again from zero.

13. Reduced to Real

You filter fortune, footnote all your hopes;
You qualify those visions born to sing;
With antidotes to brews all heaven-sent,
You dilute rapture, summarise your pain.
All tears of joy you collect in a jar;
All possibility reduced to Real.
You turn your deepest hopes to acronyms;
You live "however", "but" and "wait and see".
Thriving on the wish to thrive on nought,
You scatter all your danger on the wind.
When fire flares, a bucket lies to hand,
When passion roars, you lock the double door.
Yet when the moment takes you unawares,
You turn to raucous nova all your cares.

A sonnet on the cynicism of realism and how there's always an idealist hidden in there somewhere!

14. Cleft

Like a cleft stick,
You are no longer
Whole
See?

Yet, even
Whole,
You were ripped from
A tree.

A short poem about wholeness.
We are all part of a greater whole and can often only find meaning at a higher level
of understanding or commitment.

15. Clown Poem

Whenever he frowned
She cried.
There were tears in his eyes
She drowned;

Whenever she smiled
He frowned.
There were tears in her eyes
So he clowned.

*Sometimes we cannot bear the sadness of others; sometimes laughter can heal it. Do
you hide behind humour?
Would some humour change your perspective for the better?*

The Poetry of Change

16. The Camel Poem

"Dear momma," said the baby camel,
"Why do we have three rounded toes?"
"Well," said momma,
"Everyone knows,
for marching across the desert sand,
three toes they are just grand."

"Dear momma," said the baby camel,
"Why do we have eyelashed eyes?W
"Well," said momma,
"To keep away the biting flies."

"Dear momma," said the baby camel,
"Why do we have these humps so great?"
"Well," said momma,
"Because they are big they really ought-a
be so large to carry water."

"Dear momma," said the baby camel,
"If we are so perfect and true,
What are we doing in London Zoo?"

A poem about ultimate uniqueness. I wrote this after I heard the managing director of a failing company give a talk and say "We need to find our Unique Selling Proposition"!

17. Cat Poem

My cat became a millionaire
From all the bribes she entertained;
She hid her gold below the stair,
And sat there counting when it rained.

For though I bought her from a store,
With ragged fur and mangy paw,
Her miaow it begged for sympathy
And like a fish she had caught me!

I got her home and first the rug,
Into it her sharp claws she dug,
And then the sofa, settee, mat
Became the property of Cat.

So then the blackmail it began,
'Twas all part of her feline plan.
She howled at midnight, screeched at dawn,
She mewled and moaned across the lawn.

I never slept, the noise all night;
This once cute kitty was a blight.
She then revealed the only thing
To cease her loud feline singing:

A golden coin placed on her tail
Would cease the cataclysmic wail.
A coin would last a single day,
So soon I gave my all away.

The cat became the richest mog
And I a Paw-purr, her lap-dog.
Then one day when the coins ran out,
She stretched her legs without a shout.

The Poetry of Change

She looked at me with cold disdain,
And padded out into the rain;
And with my sack of gold in tow,
She vanished, where? I'll never know.

A poem about needy relationships.
When do needs become neediness?
Is there are balance between giving and receiving in your current relationships?

The Poetry of Change

18. The Cure

It's such a self-defeating ruse
To play the game of win and lose.

The human spirit's subtlety
Defeats all games of strategy.

A life that seeks to "reach the goals"
Creates such gaping, tawdry holes.

At night you'll wake in salted tears
Surrounded by repeating fears,

Until the day the grasping ends,
And then, see how your true heart mends.

A shoot, a bud, it rises sure.
The gentle way becomes the cure.

Often the real secret of radical change is to be gentle and patient.
How gentle are you, can you be?
When does harshness and heaviness inhibit or harm change?
When might lightness and gentleness be better?

19. Belsen

Doctor Mengele's favourite guard
Was Heinrich Edvard Braun,
For Heiny was quite diligent
And never let him down;
Yet most of all this Ober-guard,
With buttons polished new,
Had managed through a winter cold
To be civil to the Jew.

He never spoke an insult bad
Was never rude or crass,
He waved at all the children,
As they headed for the gas.
His silence was quite civil,
He never called them fools,
He hardly said a word to them,
No "Jews are animals.".
But most of our Heinrich
He knew, come end of War,
He could not be accused of hate,
For he had broke no law.

No words to hold against him.
No cry of evil stare.
He never spoke a horrid word,
No evidence was there.
Yet all the Jews in Belsen,
Remembered Heinrich most,
For his silent, distance named him,
"Dark Belsen's Cruelest Ghost".

A chilling poem about indifference.
When does indifference block change?

20. Brighton in September

You told me the tale of a lump in your breast,
Your words then fell still, and, well, I guessed the rest.

We sat in the breeze of an autumn café,
And I told you my tale of a similar day.

A lump "down below" like a ball of white snow;
The words fell again, for your eyes said "I know".

The connection is made and we laugh at those days;
It's a fine thing to feel your remembrance ablaze.

Now our lumps lie in jars for the scientists' eyes,
And each day is now such a fabulous prize.

We drank not green tea, but hot chocolate sweet,
And I noticed a dance in the toes of your feet.

A poem about life, morality, seeing the world anew, moving on. Often change involves celebrating and acknowledging the best and worst of the past, then stepping onwards.

21. The Collusion of Mediocrity

A tease.
A dance of non-
Challenge, seeking safe
Harbours at Honesty's expense.

In relief at escape
From another day's
Truth, in soothing
Saying of mock-praise,
A reward for Criticism avoided.

The collusion of mediocrity
Will please. Reward for
A neatness of nicety
To deflect the naming
Of knowing and telling it
Like it is.

A piercing look and the
True-said attack in the
Spirit of Progression.
Yet from you, no earthy
Confession. Just air.
Hot air.

I write a lot about how collusion can inhibit change. Mediocrity often results from
not being truthful, honest and risking the "zone of discomfort".
I think collusion is the biggest saboteur of change.

22. Let Go

He was full of anger and his friends told him to let it go
He was full of regret and his teacher told him to let it go
He was full of guilt and his brother told him to let it go
He was full of fear and his guide told him to let it go
He was full of anger and the eagle told him to grasp it
He was full of regret and the owl told him to look at it
He was full of guilt and the hen told him to sit on it
He was full of fear and the nightingale told him to sing to it
So he grasped it, looked at it, sat on it, and sang to it
Then the anger, regret, the guilt and fear
Let him go.

Do we really need to let go and step back, or rather take hold and go through?

23. Mouse Poem

And a chocolate racing car
Amongst the lecture notes and receipts.
The virgin Mary and the little boy Jesus
Are sheltered by a request to renew the
Boiler Insurance.

An Angel is propping up a
Visa Statement, offering it
A better balance.

Sunlight sings through the lens
Of a Glass Star of Bethlehem,
Shimmering on your Gloss Face,
Framed by plastic.

This chaos, this struggle,
A moment suspended between
The triumph of the Christmas things,
Over the reluctant recession of all
That doesn't matter any more.

A poem I wrote one Christmas. When we finally stop, at holidays times, do we ever learn to really stop. Sometimes We really do need to stop the "work" and remember that energy comes also from stillness and playfulness.

24. Thomas More

Thomas More,
He turned to me,
Without a movement of his head;
"If silence gives consent", said he,
"Then why be so weighed down with dread?"

For I may stare,
And I may brood,
These eyes intense with inward mood;
Yet, by Frick's fountain's cascade cool
I celebrate your soul, your all.

Thomas More,
He looked at me,
Without a movement of his head;
"My silence gives you full consent."
So need a single word be said?

I wrote this in New York at a visit to the Frick Collection,
an art gallery in New York.
It's based on the painting of Thomas More by Holbein. Sometimes we do not need
to say yes, or no to change. Sometimes we just need to be silent, to do or say nothing,
and given our permission for "whatever" to reveal itself.

25. The Phalanx of Cruelty

Clever words
Cradled with evil
The cult of projection
The bitterness of a lifetime
Of addiction to empty lovelessness
And abuse dressed as strength and calm
The use and abuse of language to hide shame
The worshipping of those who threaten
The love of those who laugh at pain
The erotic need for manipulation
Self-illusion and clever words
The bitterness of a lifetime
The cult of protection
Cradled with evil
Clever words

A poem about the attacking the self of another person. Sometimes we have to name and recognise forces and people who do not mean us well. Sometimes change is about resistance and protection.

26. To the Test

The fire that fiercely burns the corn,
Engendering a smoking morn,
Creates the break that stems the tide
Of forest blazes country-wide;
The molten core within your breast
Would put the Devil to the test.

Change is often about passion – passion can be angry. Sometimes we confuse passion with anger and they are not the same. Passion can be an eruption of energy, "fire in our belly".

Change can be about managing, facilitating, enabling passion and finding safer spaces to express our anger.

The Poetry of Change

27. Like A Child Again

To watch your eyes turn to golden sunrise
With each new, unravelling Christmas surprise;

To know that you are the one this time
Who opens a red stocking, as midnight bells chime;

To see complication fall momentarily away,
As you are the reason for this breaking Yuletide day;

A snow-globe shaken, a puffing circle-tree-train
So glad you're laughing like a child again.

I wrote this poem one Christmas. When we are stuck, overwhelmed, we stop using our imagination, we become close-minded and cynical. Yet the key to the change we might need lies in believing again, in become innocent and "childish" again.

28. Tears

There comes across the rainbow dawn
A gull to greet the waking morn.

There comes across the mountain high
A wise man and a lonely sigh.

There comes upon the village old
A story to keep out the cold.

There comes into a freezing bed
An arm on which to rest your head.

There comes into your crying tears
A love to clasp you through the years.

Sometimes we feel lost, paralysed, unable to change or bring about change ourselves around us. Have the courage to just be open, to wait with hope, not expectation. Often then, all kinds of resources and help come towards us.

The Poetry of Change

29. Back Here

I remember sitting here before;
Remembering I had sat here before,
Promising I would never find
Myself back here, sitting and
Remembering.
This voice
Can no longer utter a sentence
Without a coffee-laden, smoky wheeze.
These movements are slower now,
More clumsy,
Though perhaps they are the same
As before, and it is
This place
That has become clumsier and slower.
Is this the last time
I will sit here,
Lost in memory?
Taking a cappuccino?
Or will this place come once again
To me, unbidden,
As so many times before?
This time,
Will you come,
As you did, that first time,
A hay cart loaded with
Curiosity and irresistible Accusations?

*I wrote this on a return trip to France. Sometimes our future can only come about if
we revisit the past.
Sometimes the clues to what lies ahead, lies in what lies behind.
The word "before" can mean in front of us (before us)
and also behind us (what went before).*

30. Cause and Effect

In real love,
We are neither cause nor effect,
Force nor motive.
We neither own nor need;
We are simple, we are gentle;
The fire that crackles,
Comes from no lit touchpaper,
But from the molten core
That metamorphoses freedom into play;
It's fashioned of aeons, breathed in, in moments;
Eyes light up, not with push or pull,
But with the ever-knowing of the self's true freedom;
We neither own nor need,
We are one, as a deed.
I'll not try to win you,
For the victory is not mine, it is ours.

Change involves letting go. Sometimes – not always – the ego gets in the way.
Sometimes it is about we-ness, not I-ness, the community not the individual.
Do you know how to really collaborate? When does your ego get in the way? When
should you assert your needs more forcefully?

31. Floorboards

Slowly, seeping in
Unnoticed under
The floorboards;
The level rises until your
Carpet of Comfort is sodden
The level rises
Flooding your defences,
Drenching your things.

The water will come to claim
What you accepted so readily;
So easily you received,
Then slammed shut the Gate
And bolted your doors.

Now it creeps upon you
Reclaiming the inches,
Each drop of this deluge
Is one of the tears
Cried by the ones who
Gave with such hopes.

Then comes a new flood
To rise up and drown you
The tears of the moments
You lost in your locking;
Each tear was a gift that
Your meanness forbade you
To give in return.

Now water is rising
It reaches the roof
And claims all the bricks
That you built in your fear.

The Poetry of Change

A cleansing, a drowning,
Returning to soil,
And that ground is remade
On a landscape of tears.

A poem about change overwhelming us.

This often happens when we let things build up, fester, until we get flooded, taken over.
When is it better to be direct and not suppress what you are really feeling?
Is it time to deal with an issue you are putting off dealing with?

The Poetry of Change

32. The Gift

Words they will not serve to heal the fears;
Impossible to understand this dark,
Forbidding field of memory-laden tears;
A wish to find a spirit-golden spark

The wheel will turn and turn again it will,
And wrong to right will find its way to you.
Into the void a light begins to fill,
Like summer sun on icy morning dew.

The shadow cast it, calls you to the fight,
To look ahead with crazy diamond glare,
To stand before the ghosts beside a knight,
Who meets the foe with equal angry stare.

The future is a place that can be touched;
The past the dark's domain but it is past.
It's time to slay the dragon, oh that such
As you can have a joy that's born to last.

That joy it comes to meet us from a place
Called Future into Present it doth sound;
A day to heal for all in you is grace,
For you did plant your life in fertile ground.

The void it is a place, so dark secure,
But joy and fun and laughter is your right;
So take this gift, all wrapped in words of love,
A greeting call to find your golden light.

*A traditional style poem, with a bit of an epic feel – this explores finding our
spark – the spark the might be needed to light the fire that makes change happen*

The Poetry of Change

33. The Trumpet

We do not need to trumpet our lives,
Like desperate Hollywood husbands and wives;

We have no need to share our secret names
Online, to fan these decaying, lovelorn flames.

We do not need to talk down the walk of tears
To flee the climb of freedom through the years.

This is a poem about playing out your private life on social media.
Change, I believe, is often sacred, precious, vital. Sometimes we have to let it simmer
and mature inside of us.
We don't always have to be an open book.

34. Mermaid

When you dance,
You step like a mermaid
On the pain of ground.

Once your pain showed
In those moments when
You weren't dancing.

The golden chain
Lit up your dancer-eyes
For a moment.

Then it was gone.

I am no maestro.
Yet I will search my
Remaining days for a
Song that will
Set you to dancing
Again.

A poem about finding the way back, often with the help of someone else. Sometimes we can't fix it for ourselves and there is no help we can pay for. Sometimes it is our friends and loved ones who are the agents of our positive change.

35. The Part Of Me

The part of me that
Holds your hand
Is a part that laughs at haughty ways;
It holds the world on fingertips
It fixes such a steady gaze.

Its door can never close for it
Was opened by a thing of light;
It's panoramic sweep of wings
Transcends this pain, ensouls the sight.

The part of me that
Holds your hand
Has walked through Death's appalling vale,
And found there beauty in the dark
And spun from it a healing tale.

The page it turns, papyrus cream,
It shares with you a single dream;
The letters set by you so clear
Are words that put to flight all fear.

The part of me that
Holds your hand
Is sure, and firm, and never fails,
A calm ship on your sea of change.
With golden prow and pure, white sails.

This is a poem about recognising when we could benefit from a mentor, from being helped, advised, guided by someone who has greater experience of life than we have.

The Poetry of Change

36. On Ditchling Beacon

We melted into the meadow
And wild grasses tickled us
Even as we chased each other.
You can see the planes
At Gatwick from here
On a clear day, and no day
Was ever as wonderfully clear as this.
You told me fairy tales of
Light and Shadow, and I knew
This was the Story of You.
You told me your plans
As if they were myths and legends of old.
And, up here, I believed them all.
Witches used to dance here, love,
Under moon-skies on windy nights;
The wolves were running then, but not today
As we held each other, high on Ditchling Beacon.

*One of my favourite poems about meeting nature, and meeting each other in nature
– in that part of nature that borders on human place. Sometimes we need to find a
high place – literally – to get a higher view of change. Where could you go, near
where you live, to get an "over"-view?*

The Poetry of Change

37. Slovenian Sunset

Do you understand how powerful
A gentle sunset can be?
Do you ever feel the magical force
Of not-needing-to-try?
This golden, maroon-wash
Is an is-ness that calls forth no strategy.
It settles for its own soft delight;
And, without an act,
Lays down its challenge to you,
To finally find your gentle self;
The self that moves the cliff-face
Without so much as a glancing touch.
It whispers: "Drop your patterning.
Enjoy the emergent happening."

*A poem about sunsets, emergence and how the end of the day is the perfect time to
let go.
How easy do you find it to let go?
Can you surrender to the moment and see what emerges?*

The Poetry of Change

38. A Gift of Angels

I send you love from this fine place,
My stars are touching your fair face;
A realm of light, adorns your sight,
I'm flying now, above your night!
My tears are raindrops fresh and clear,
They wash you clean, they calm your fear,
And when you search for hope from woe
I'll be with you, and help you grow.

"I am the moon that lights your way;
I am the sun that greets your day;
I am the laugh that salves your pain;
I am your cooling summer rain."
I'm gliding now on wings of light;
My soul is free and burning bright.
A cascade pure, a guiding star;
Remember, love, I'm never far.

I'm soaring now above the skies,
So let not tears fill up your eyes.
My daughter fair, please hear my rune,
Live well, and weave your gorgeous tune.
And when each day, sun rises new,
On angels wings, I fly to you
As silver waves they kiss the shore,
I step into your life once more.

I wrote this poem, rather suddenly, for a friend who had lost a close relative. It's about how those we lose can live on in different ways. We all have different beliefs about what happens after "death". In this poem, whether in memory, or behaviour in life, or in genuine continuity of spirit, those we love can live on in and with us. Change is always transition to something else.

39. Pale

There is a red-golden sunset
Reflected in these tears;
It's a sunset the colour of watercascade hair
And pale skin that hides a furnace
Upon which fierce dreams are forged.

A poem about sunset, loss and passion. Sometimes the way out of a difficult situation comes from the process of reflection.

40. A Moment Into Black

The curses came through window panes of grey,
Cast cackles of disdain upon the fire.
Around the hearth sat warming hands and toes,
In cloaks of crimson, purple, jaunty green.
Such stories told, such verse was freely shared!
And wine aplenty hot from spicy brews.
A voice, the teller sang a wondrous tale;
Yet from the shadows came the angry imps.
They smashed the cups and pissed upon the flames.
They tore with daggers into cooling cheeks;
They ripped an eye and kicked into a groin.
The circle broke a moment into black;
But then our eyes they met in strength of will,
Remade the circle, banished all the chill.

A sonnet looking at spoilers and cynics in life, and how a strong group can become powerful at upholding an important goal or vision together

41. At Rosslyn

A rare sun is exploding
Over Edinburgh,
Showering the seekers
With a a tartan lattice of shadow and light,
Overlaying the criss-crossing of
Grey stone cobbled lanes and climbs.

These seekers after songs and jigs,
Theatrics and laughter, with a dram
To warm a too-early Autumn evening.
Fireworks are bursting over the castle again,
The pipes are playing, and you are smiling again,
Because today you touched the Holy Grail at Rosslyn.

This was a day trip, and escape in the middle of the noise of the Edinburgh Festival; an escape and an insight. Rosslyn Chapel is a very mysterious place in Scotland. I go there every year, spend some time reflecting, and always come back with new thoughts and ideas. It can be an old place, somewhere in nature, even a park in the centre of a busy city – where do you go to get unique thoughts about change?

42. A Healing Verse

Sun-warming, flowing
Nerves to natural song.
Dancing rhythm
From heart to fingertips.

Spirits of Movement
Touching me with their
Soft, healing hands.
I find the enlivening,
Clear horizon within me.

This is a verse that can be used for meditation when you need to heal – physically, emotionally, spiritually. It is spiritual in style but not religious.

43. Into this Place

In this place there are only tones.
No bodily function yet movement
From thought that flexes
Non-existent muscles.
There are no nouns, only verb
Upon verb, Like fields and valleys,
The language spoken by
The dead, who have cast off all nouns
Is a landscape uttered here.
There are harmonics and rising pitch
That discords as pain, and accords
As love.
In this place there is only tone.
There is communion in notes with a
Melody of Meaning and it is possible
To touch another with the intention
Of a healing song.
Into this place, I unfold my wings of sound-borne light.

Sometimes spoken and written words get in the way of communication. Sometimes change comes about better when we are more "embodied" - when we don't speak, but when we move, when we gesture, when we relate in ways other than our brains. There are lots of ways to do this – you can find approaches in the arts, in the world of theatre, dance, in yoga and practices such as contact improvisation. Why not try a non-verbal way to experience change?

The Poetry of Change

44. Angels

When you fired your mortar
At a child,
Did you know that
An Angel cried?

Enfolding both she and
Her trembling uncle
In astral winds?

Your metallic fist
Thrust aside the
Protective fold,
Opened its fingers
And took the child's
Tiny hand even as it
Reached for her
Surrogate papa.
Was it only that
Wispy clasp
Of protective love
That shunned the projectile
Deflecting it
From her growing heart?

And the angel cried.
"We have come to close
To the Earth. And
Our wings are spread too thinly."

I wrote this poem during the war in the former Yugoslavia. I wrote it from the safety of Zagreb. It's written from the imagined perspective of an angel but it is really a poem about how taking a "higher" view can not be enough to change something for the better. Sometimes we have to get "down here" and take action.

The Poetry of Change

45. I Fear the Silence

I fear the silence now,
I cover my skin with television
And radio noise.
I surround my silence with book
Upon book upon book;
Even music has too much silence in it,
For the pictures call out
To be made by me; out of my silence.
So each tune, is accompanied by silent television
And a book.
And I fear the silence now.
The sound of the wind, the rattle of the rain
Is too silent so
I cover my skin with television
And radio noise.
I never feared it before, but
I fear the silence now.

Many people these days are uneasy with silence. We are used to the noise of a media-loaded world. In silence we can hear our own thoughts – our fears and insecurities. It's easy to fill that silence with content, with conversation. Yet much change – perhaps the change we really need, involves us risking silence. Out of the silence comes real possibility.

46. In Wildness Anew

For to mend
with a scowl
and an anger-borne
fist for those who
insist on
putting to swift
Death
the scorn of your foes.
A feather-soft
breath to
tease you to flight
of a floating relief
on a breeze to be
borne on the might of your dreams
of such daring respite.
And it seems
I will oft steal your
sadness – a thief
in the night
Then with zeal I will bear it aloft.
Then will you feel
only that which seeks
how to prove
that your sadness, though true
in the pale of your cheeks
Cannot fail to
remake you in wildness
Anew.

*Read this one aloud! It's about how we can remake ourselves – sometimes quickly
and in dramatic ways. Sometimes change is wild, sudden and big.*

The Poetry of Change

47. It Rises

Night doesn't fall here;
It rises.
There's a place near your door
Where moonlight touches
A water cascade.

You have such a soft, simple, smile;
Like rocks teased by aeons of
A silvery stream's lazy intention.
We're the night now.

Our eyes are stars,
Supping on moon-milk,
And sparkling like diamonds,
Made in the heat of far planets' cores.

A sudden clear picture of another soul sits at the core of this short poem. We sometimes say a person is "on another planet" and yet change is all about encountering the alien, the mystery of other people and situations.

48. Train Poem

You are pushing the end of your carriage
In a vain attempt to move the train.
And you are on the inside.
The random lurch convinces you that
God is on your side and that your
Fortuitous forward journey was meant to be.
There will be no stops on this express ride
to destruction. Headlong you will steam,
Toot-tooting to the people on passing platforms.
They are not waving, they are warning!
Downhill, plunging at ninety an hour, the
Looks of loving concern are a blur of
Indifferent encouragement. This train will be
Mightily early for a destination that is an eternity
Beyond the end of these old rails.

Sometimes we are the cause of our own downfall. We are not always in control and sometimes admitting that and seeking help, pausing and reflecting is the first step to avoiding disaster?
Who could you go to for help?
Who would you listen to if they told you to slow down or stop?

49. Cream Tea

I only wish you could make sense
Of this jaded, failing eloquence.
When we are sitting eye to eye,
There is no need to even try.

Upon the page, with pen in hand,
These words, so clumsy, mark the sand.
The self-same heart, that aims so well,
Trips on itself and falls to Hell.

The breath that speaks a kindly word,
In ink reduces to absurd.
So please imagine lips not page,
And look for tears, and not for rage.

I only wish you could make sense
Of this jaded, fading eloquence.
This voice, it whispers a soft prayer,
In hope you'll hear what's truly there.

*Sometimes we have to listen beyond the words. People often stumble over what they
are trying to say. Often we regret our words.
How tolerantly and generously do you listen to others?
Have you jumped to conclusions?*

The Poetry of Change

50. Cream Tea

Will there ever come a time
When all my wildest dreams have gone?
When there is too much raspberry jam
And not enough cream to dress my scone?

Will the knife that is my life
Always spread itself too thin?
Will the tart that is my heart
Spill out crumbs upon my chin?

And when my life is done
And I must fly into the sun,
Will I wish that I could take
Just one extra slice of cake?

I wrote this lyrical poem on the day I went to celebrate the news that I had been cured of Testicular Cancer (I was 30 years old). I celebrated with a cream tea at the Mock Turtle Tea Shop. When change is successful, we should always celebrate and reflect.

The End

If you'd like to read more of Paul Levy's writings, visit his web site:

www.cats3000.com

Printed in Great Britain
by Amazon.co.uk, Ltd.,
Marston Gate.